SHAPES AROUND M

Circles

Anita Loughrey

QED

What is a circle?

This is a circle. A circle is a round shape with no corners.

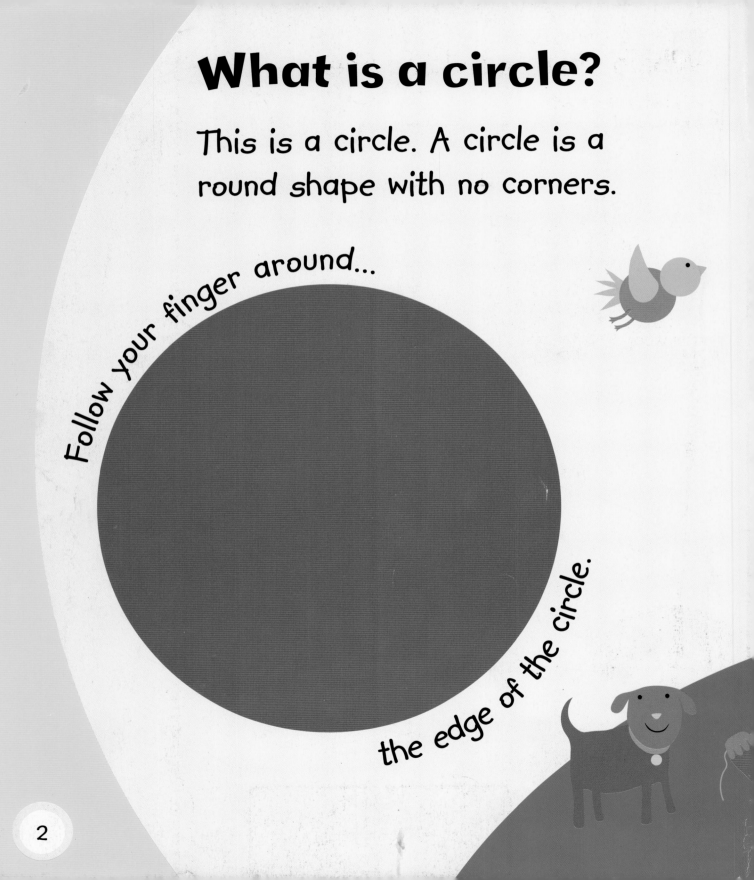

Follow your finger around...

the edge of the circle.

Which child is holding the circle kite?

Sam　　　　**John**　　　　**Jenny**

3

Answer: John

Counting circles

Point to the circles in the pictures.

How many circles does the caterpillar's body have?

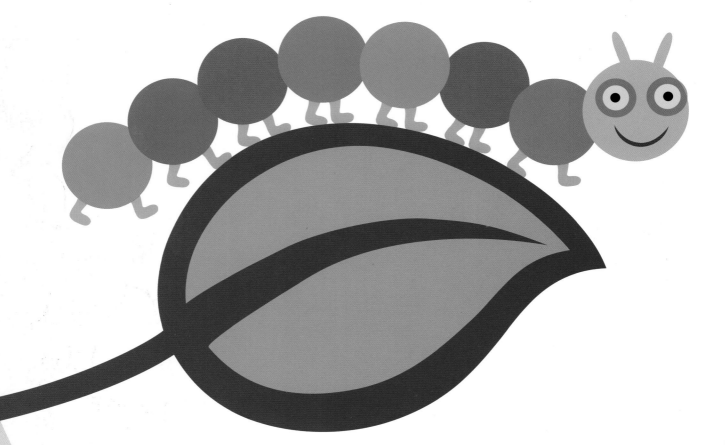

Answer: 7 circles

Look out of the window. Can you see any circle shapes?

How many yellow circles does the flower have?

5

Answer: 6 circles

Big and small

Circles can *be different sizes.*

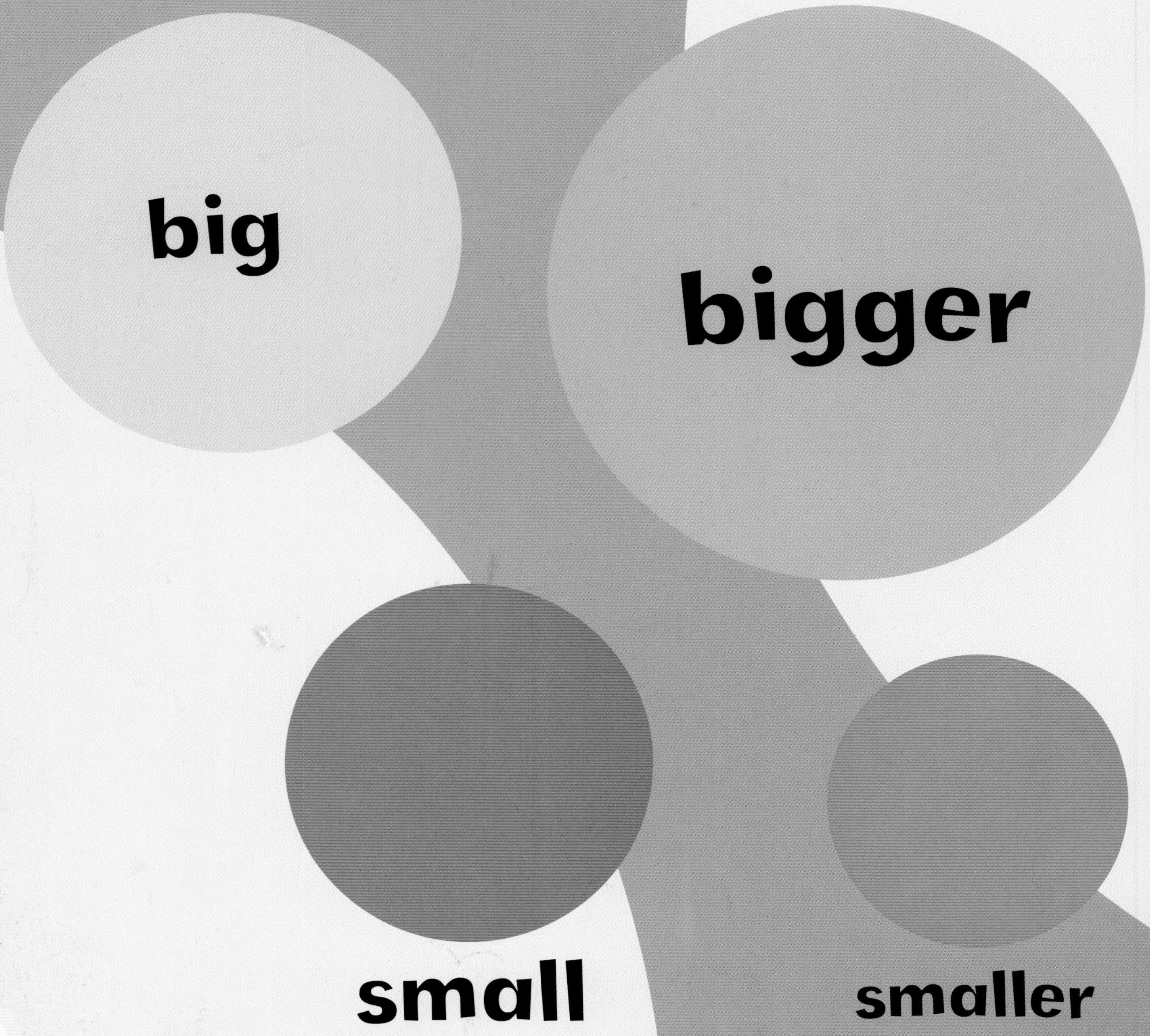

big

bigger

small

smaller

biggest

Look around your house. Can you find a big circle shape?

smallest

Coloured circles

Circles can be different colours.

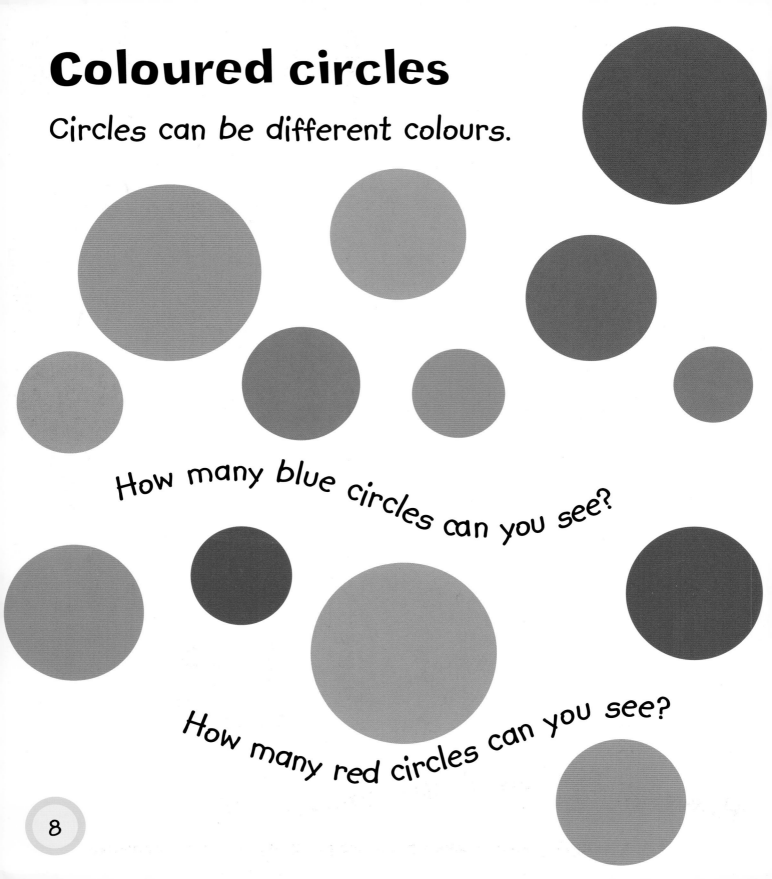

How many blue circles can you see?

How many red circles can you see?

8

How many green circles can you see?

How many yellow circles can you see?

Answers: 3 blue circles, 2 red circles, 3 green circles, 5 yellow circles

Caterpillar crazy!

Help the caterpillar follow the path to get to the cabbage patch.

How many circles does the caterpillar pass?

Drawing circles

Ask an adult to help you to draw this plate of cakes.

Ask an adult to help
you to draw these
plates of pizza.

In the sandpit

Point to the circles in the picture.
Can you spot them all?

bucket

sun

sunhat

Which of these circles can you find when you play in the sand?

ice cream

sunglasses

wheel

shell

In the kitchen

Point to the circles
in the picture. Which
circles are small?

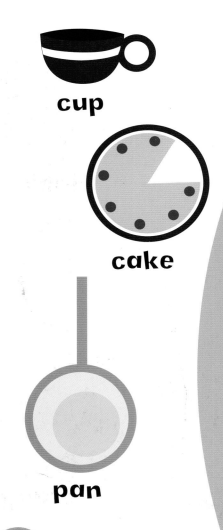

cup

cake

pan

What circles can you see in your kitchen?

clock

plate

orange

17

the playground

Point to the circles
in the picture.
Which ones have
you played with?

football

tyre

basketball

Which of these circles can you find in your playground?

roundabout

tennis racket

hoop

In the garden

Point to the circles in the picture. Which circle is the biggest?

umbrella

apple

hosepipe

Can you find any circle shapes in your garden?

bird table

flower

plant pot

21

In the street

Point to all the circles in the picture. Can you see them all?

balloon

button

sign

22

Can you find these circle shapes in your street?

watch

traffic light

steering wheel

Notes for parents and teachers

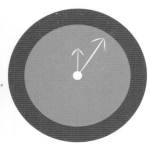

This book has been designed to help your child recognize circles and to distinguish them from other shapes. The emphasis is on making learning fun, so the book uses the environment to reinforce what your child has seen in the book. The activities help your child to understand the idea of a circle shape by using familiar, everyday objects.

Sit with your child and read each page to them. Allow time for your child to think about the activity. Encourage them to talk about what they see. Praise your child when they recognize the items shown in the book from their own experience. If any of the items are unfamiliar to your child, talk about them and explain what they are and where they might be found. Whenever possible, provide opportunities for your child to see the items in the everyday world around them.

Other activities for you to try with your child are:

✳ Play games such as, 'I spy with my little eye something circle shaped that begins with...'.

✳ Cut out pictures of different-shaped objects from a catalogue and ask your child to sort them by shape, or to match them to pictures in this book.

✳ Encourage your child to look for things that are circle shaped when you are out and about, or play this game at home.

✳ Let your child make collages or junk-models of different circle objects, or mould them in clay, so that they can explore the shape by touch.

Remember to keep it fun. Stop before your child gets tired or loses interest and try again another day. Children learn best when they are relaxed and enjoying themselves. It is best to help them to experience new concepts in small steps, rather than to try to do too much at once.

Illustrator: Sue Hendra
Editor: Amanda Askew
Designer: Susi Martin

Educational consultant:
Jillian Harker

Copyright © QED Publishing 2010

First published in the UK in 2010 by
QED Publishing
A Quarto Group company
226 City Road
London ECIV 2TT

www.qed-publishing.co.uk

ISBN 978 1 84835 472 2

Printed in China